This book is lovingly dedicated to both my daughter Teresa and my niece Ruth, whose untiring help made it possible.

Miriam Brown

LIGHT AND DARK:
POEMS AND STORIES

AUSTIN MACAULEY PUBLISHERS™
LONDON • CAMBRIDGE • NEW YORK • SHARJAH

Copyright © Miriam Brown 2023

The right of Miriam Brown to be identified as author of this work has been asserted by the author in accordance with sections 77 and 78 of the Copyright, Designs and Patents Act 1988.

All rights reserved. No part of this publication may be reproduced, stored in a retrieval system, or transmitted in any form or by any means, electronic, mechanical, photocopying, recording, or otherwise, without the prior permission of the publishers.

Any person who commits any unauthorised act in relation to this publication may be liable to criminal prosecution and civil claims for damages.

A CIP catalogue record for this title is available from the British Library.

ISBN 9781035811618 (Paperback)
ISBN 9781035811625 (Hardback)
ISBN 9781035811632 (ePub e-book)

www.austinmacauley.com

First Published 2023
Austin Macauley Publishers Ltd®
1 Canada Square
Canary Wharf
London
E14 5AA

I acknowledge with gratitude the support I received from Lyn Darrant, Robert Crick, Frances Deegan, Cathy Kelly, Anne Everest-Phillips, Valerie Bettag, Jeremy Burchardt, Jennifer Jannaway and the late Kingsley Squire.

Table of Contents

Introduction	11
Of Alma Bridge – Sidmouth	12
Of the Incoming Tide – Worthing	13
Evening in the City – London	14
The Sea – Sidmouth	15
Canada – Reflections in Ontario	16
Quebec – Reflections in the Mountains	17
Rhesus Factor? – Right, Monkey!	18
There They Sit	19
Most Admirable Oranges	20
In the Mire	21
Simple Simon	22
Wail	23
Tea and Beer	24
PIG	26
The Turkish Water Fan Cat	27
Artefact	28
Fable	29
Rich Grandma	30
The Unsaid Goodbye	31

Bike	**33**
Housewife	**34**
Monday Morning	**36**
Born to Be King?	**37**
Seventy-Seventh Birthday	**38**
When Doubts Ignored	**39**
At Ladram Bay	**41**
To the Poet Dylan Thomas	**42**
The Pacifist	**43**
The Second Coming	**44**
The Phoenix	**45**
Treacle	**46**
Her Hair as Flames	**48**
Night	**49**
When Images	**50**
Where Are You, My Love	**51**
Just Once	**52**
Peace Not War	**53**
Pollution	**55**
Wealth and Poverty	**57**
A Glass of Beer	**58**
Nature	**59**
Song of Mixed Race	**60**
Our Angel Now In Heaven	**61**

To Teresa	62
A Ball of Fire	63
FRENCH POEMS	65
Poème 1	66
Poem 1	67
Poème 2	68
Poem 2	69
Poème 3	70
Poem 3	71
Poème 4	72
Poem 4	73
Poème 5	74
Poem 5	75
Poème 6	76
Poem 6	77
Poème 7	78
Poem 7	79
STORIES	81
A Coroner's Verdict	83
What If	85
The Underworn Underwear	86
The Underwired Bra	87
Thirteen Minutes Past One	88
Unfinished Business	89

Funny Face Betty	90
The Curtain Twitch'd	94
The Break with Tradition	99
Confession	103
Message in a Bottle	105

Introduction

Miriam was born in London, but evacuated to Sussex early in World War Two. She began writing poems and stories at aged 17, and continued doing so while training as a nurse in Brighton. Canada fascinated her, and her stay there has influenced both her English and French poetry. She includes a translation of her seven little French poems. Miriam now lives in Sidmouth and is still writing poetry. Her poems have won prizes in Sidmouth Literary Festival.

Of Alma Bridge

Sidmouth

The morning sun at Alma Bridge
Awakes my soul with joy this day
But oh, I feel so sad to see
Those lovely cliffs that ridge on ridge
Do slither, crumble to the sea
And leave great gaps with mounds of scree.

Refreshing breezes gently waft
On Sidmouth Esplanade at dusk
And now the cliffs appear so soft
As glowing rose with light-and hush
Such tiny waves spread foam like frost,
While Earth halts its bewildered rush.

2016

Of the Incoming Tide

Worthing

The wheeling seagulls scream for joy
The vicious salty wind
Cuts clean upon my face – Hurrah!
The tide is coming in!

Across rippling flats the white waves stream
Hard driven into shore
And dashed upon the shining shingle
Smash and hiss for more –

The slashing gale, the crashing sea –
I shout and join the din
The seagulls shriek in frenzy – and
The tide is *racing* in!

1954

Evening in the City

London

See down the arid crawling city street
The office buildings throbbing in the glow –
Fiery windows like a row of suns
All setting in the softened autumn gold
Of evening.

High up on infinite blue
Swift strokes of whitewash hang against the sky –
Brittle, fragile, scarcely even there.
Joyful breezes in their well-trained way
Go straight about their airy business.

Far beyond the dampened east, a world
From children's story books, of built up cloud
Conceals a giant's fortress, caves and woods
Where strange and dim a Holy Grail might hide
And witches weave their spells, though not in Time....

1966

The Sea

Sidmouth

Mists hang limp on glass green billows
Smoothly, gently undulating
Green from softest greys emerging
Merging with a dark horizon.
Gracious rosy cliffs reach skyward
Crowned with darkest trees and foliage.
Pebbles each has its allurement
Each by mighty glaciers sculpted
Shining each in varied colour
Washed by tides through countless ages.
Creamy foam slips through the pebbles
Hiss, retreats, then rushes onward.
Blissful healing soothes the spirit
Joyful hope fills all the senses
Anxious thoughts evaporating
Time suspended in this moment.

2016

Canada

Reflections in Ontario

Oh, it's Hiawatha country, with the
Great rough lumps of rock
And great wide sky above the sheets of lake
Where pine trees raise their arms to beckon
Ragged rain – clouds grey
That trail their misty muslin as they break

The land of Minnehaha, she whose
Name is Laughing Water,
Where streams splash brightly, pierced by spears of gold,
Or vast and clean and icy green
Cool lakes serenely lap
At wrinkled mossy rocks, worn kind and old.

1961

Quebec

Reflections in the Mountains

The rainclouds hang like scrappy bits of rag
About the spikes of pines at St. Laurant.
The drizzle beats like childish rage in vain,
Then tiring soon weeps quietly to sleep.
The humid summer's gone, and hot gold fall,
Now winter snows and wolves shall softly come.

'Snow!' children shout in joy, and paint their sledge,
Lights in their eyes and in their modern homes.
The well-insured young parents move the car
To fetch the double windows from the shed.
Old people hug their thinning coats again
And wait for street cars in the stiff grey slush,
While everyone is seeking in the stores
Expensive useless gifts for Christmas Day.

But June shall come, with shifting veils of rain
Drifting, trailing, mingling on the lakes –
Lakes vast and clean and icy green and cool
Among the wrinkled mossy time-worn rocks
Where tall dark pine trees raise their arms to greet
The great wide skies beyond the open seas,
And puffy cloudlets wand'ring slowly by
The prairie-lands and mountains of the West.

1960

Rhesus Factor? – Right, Monkey!

When this terrestrial globe was young
And so was Father Time
We tried our little oozy best
Evolving from the slime.
Respectable a citizen
As you, sir, and as me
Must radically disturbing find
This fact – if fact it be.
At any rate, see for yourself,
It isn't in your bible –
I really think we might, by George,
Have boffins sued for libel!

1953

(In 1953 the 'Rhesus factor', found in the blood of humans and the Rhesus monkey, was being much discussed, and 'Right, Monkey' was a catch phrase in a popular radio comedy series.)

There They Sit

Big and fat
Satisfied
Smug and that
Faces bright,
Silly grin
I could prick
With a pin.
Pompously
There they squat
Oranges –
Cheeky lot!

1953

Most Admirable Oranges

Most admirable oranges
From California's bower
0 kind and gracious oranges
Sunkist from hour to hour
Most condescending oranges
Antithesis of sour – I crave you!

Magnificent, illustrious
And ancient is your name;
Unparalleled and glorious
Is your undying fame;
What matter you're too stout to walk –
You roll around the same! I squeeze you!

O great and worthy oranges
Upon your noble brow
I'd place a wreath of laurels and
Perform a seemly bow
But your hairline has receded and
I can't quite figure how! I suck you!

1956

('Sunkist' used to be a brand of orange at the time this poem was written.)

In the Mire

Economic growth and credit
Could not last forever
We always knew they'd have to end
Despite Man's best endeavour
We knew the bubble had to burst
'Twas more than just a hunch
And soon we'll all be in the mire
They call it 'Credit Crunch'.

Predictably this has to be
Followed by inflation
Or is it something we'll endure
As better than stagnation?
At any rate we're in a mess
And are we in the mire?
The handiwork of governments,
Until we all expire!

2012

Simple Simon

Simple Simon saw a pie shop
Somewhere near the Market Square
If the pie is nice and hot
It cost him more, which is unfair.

It's a government tradition
Losing popularity
Start a war, or silly tax
Causing wide hilarity.

What the government would like,
Distracting all the blame from them
Is workers on a general strike
The country split and in mayhem.

2012

Wail

We hear so much about men's egos –
Goodness will they ever stop!
The poor exquisite darling creatures –
Heavens, sure my brain will pop!
They are so occupied with pride
And want to take you – for a ride!
We hear so much about poor men –
Goodness, I shan't bother, then!

1969

Tea and Beer

I never watch sport on the news
It's not my cup of tea,
Though sport is good for one's physique
I'm sure you will agree.
When young I played at tennis
But I always missed the ball,
And running round to find it
Bored my friends – I lost them all!
I much preferred the hockey field,
'Twas my idea of fun
To whack the shins of other girls
Until somebody won.
But swimming was my greatest joy
I dived from the top board,
Though only once – a belly flop –
And I felt that I'd scored!
I biked up Chanctonbury Ring
Except for fifty yard –
It's nearly vertical you know
And consequently hard.
The view is quite phenomenal
And cycling down is great,
Whilst bumping over flint stones
The rims hot from the brake.
Sometimes I tried my hand at darts,
With siblings, at a pub,
A lady bobbed on tiptoes, screamed,
Her dart aimed at the hub;
The dart then left her shaking hand
And weaving through the air
It landed safely on the floor –
Sighs of relief we shared!

I did my best at Judo
With considerable success,
Though I refused my yellow belt
'Cos women win for less.
Now, when I hear that Hibs have won,
I give a hearty cheer
That someone else has scored a goal –
I'm here just for the beer!

2010

(For those who don't know, 'Hibs' is Hibernian Edinburgh football team.)

PIG

The pig he stood upon the road
Around the bend he stood
He watched the traffic whizzing by
And unconcerned he stood.

The hedges they were very high
The bends were very tight
But piggy loved to watch the cars
As they sped into sight.

He watched the lorries roaring past
As they swung round the bend
His joy was great, as was his fate –
He had a bacon end!

2007

The Turkish Water Fan Cat

Magnificent his fluffy tail
Marmalade in hue
The rest of him is snowy white,
His forehead orange, too.

He curls up in a tiny ball
And kicks and spits and scratches
So Roger wears a gardening glove
For gladiatorial matches.

At least, that used to be the case
When Chester was a kitten,
Then came a time when puss was ill,
By fox or badger bitten!

For weeks he lay a sorry cat
On life-supporting drip –
He's well now, though he's fatter,
Less inclined to scratch and nip

No longer does he walk the roofs
With nine and ninety lives,
He only plunders neighbours' ponds –
Not one gold fish survives!

So Chester's epitaph might be
'Here lies a naughty cat
Whose lives eventually ran out –
He died, and that was that.'

2004

Artefact

The small tree seems diminished by
Its balls of gold and red
It came from 'Save the Children' shop,
Priced at 'Two Pound' it said.

From where does it originate?
Perhaps a foreign factory
And then brought here by aeroplane?
Not very satisfactory.

From what materials was it made?
There's nothing here to say –
It stands on three feet, not on four,
But balances okay.

So 'Thank you' to the man or girl
Who made my little tree.
I hope that it is never 'dumped',
It means so much to me.

But if you've noticed only
Its balls of red and green
Just ask it now, 'Dear little tree
What has your story been,

And what is to become of you
When you're no longer needed?'
The humble thing might well reply,
'The joy I gave succeeded!'

2007

Fable

A little mouse sat in her hole
But near her hole no bread crumbs lay
She languished there for want of food
And crouched in fear, day after day.

One morn some crumbs were left nearby
''Tis good,' said she, 'my fortunes change.'
She ate and rallied, shone her eye,
Saw other corners, greater range.

Her little friends advised her,
'Go into that corner over there
For often crumbs are left behind.
Far happier, and better fare.'

The little mouse felt better now,
She'd eaten and regained her strength,
'But things are better now,' she said.
She stayed, and there she died at length.

1969

Rich Grandma

Want to give the kids some fun
There won't be much left when I'm gone.
If I'm careful, practice thrift,
I'd like to make a Christmas gift
Trainers and a Barbie doll –
Counting pennies takes its toll.
Meals from Tesco don't cost much –
Computer games? I'm out of touch
Music always has its fashions –
Healthy eating, watch the rations –
Ought to pay the monthly rent
How much this week have I spent?
David's in a local gang
Sandra's always using slang
People call it 'street-wise jargon'
No-one says 'I beg your pardon' –
Can't keep up, I'm nearly crying,
This old girl on the block is dying.

2012

The Unsaid Goodbye

A school fete
Autumn 1957 I suppose
So long ago I can't be sure
It was Saturday –
A Saturday afternoon
A bit cloudy and windy
And getting late.

I lost sight of her for a moment
Her anxious little face
And auburn frizzy hair –
I reckon she was six then.

But I saw her again through the mêlée.
She still looked strained, concerned –
Frightened.
Although partially relieved
When she noticed me.
'What's wrong?' I asked.
I tried to reach her
But the crowd pressed her backwards
Small anxious face peering at me
Pleading.
Scared.
Then she was gone.

Nearby a dark steamship began to struggle against the tide
It found its way along a channel
Until I could no longer see it.
Yes, she was gone.

Who is this Mrs. Delaney?
She looked at me curiously – severely –
Long skirt, chignon, spectacles,
Riding away on an upright bicycle and
Staring at me over her shoulder –
A long, hard glance.

Gradually the cloud cover darkened everything,
And the evening light faded.
But I could only stand there.

2012

Bike

'But, Mum, they all go fast,' he said,
Face radiant with joy.
She saw her nineteen-year-old son.
She saw a little boy.

'But, Mum, I've got the gear,' he said,
'I really have to go.'
'All right dear, do take care then,'
And a kiss at the door and so

She heard the bike 'rev up' outside,
She heard him ride away.
Somehow she knew she'd never see
Her son beyond that day.

'Can you identify him please, Madam?
The end was very quick.'
The woman spoke, she merely said,
'He'd…had…the…bike…one…week!'

2007

Housewife

Mrs Black and Mrs White
Working morning, noon and night
Got to make the house quite tidy!
Else he'll give you such a hiding
Though you're pregnant, scarcely able
Meals must be upon the table.
Though you've post-natal depression
His welfare is his obsession.

See his weekly pay pack bulging –
Most of it for his indulging
Beer and women at the pub.
Top yourself? 'Aye, there's the rub.'
Kids must always be looked after,
Must not guess life is disaster
Hide the bruises, hide the pain,
Kids come first, that's always plain.

Mrs Black and Mrs White
Hold your head up, walk upright
When you're shopping and you're seen,
Mustn't be a drama queen.
Pride is precious, don't give way –
What would all the neighbours say!

He's come home – why – it's too early,
Ominously looking surly
Growling that he's 'got the sack,'
It's your fault, he'll pay you back.

Stiff with bruises crawl to bed
Every night until you're dead!

Mrs White and Mrs Black
Work or husband break your back
No respite until you die –
No-one knows or cares but I.

2014

Monday Morning

Monday, and he's at the office.
Took the kids to school as promised,
Pushed the Hoover round the corners –
Whoops, it's sucked up John's pyjamas,
Knocked the photos off the shelf,
Wedding day of him and self
School photos, us in our teens
Shattered all to smithereens!

Yank the Hoover through the door
Plug it in again once more –
Now of course it doesn't work,
I gave it such a hearty jerk.
What to do? No-one to aid,
And still the beds have not been made.

The kitten's made another puddle –
Everything's a frightful muddle,
Washing piled up on the floor,
Ironing from the week before,
Baby's screaming, must be fed –
Post-natal blues – wish I were dead.

I'm sure I'm going really crazy –
Oh please God make me rich and lazy!

2014

Born to Be King?

He'd never be a useful king
He'd never make decisions
He'd falter and he'd dither, yes,
With righteous imprecisions

He'd listen to his ministers
They'd vie with one another
They'd try to flatter him, of course,
And call each other 'Brother'.

But when it comes to making laws
The point of legislation
Is 'What's in it for me and thee?
Impoverish the nation!'

The only point of going to war
Is filling up the coffers
'Those in the vanguard get more praise –
Here, line up with your offers!'

Look, see this dagger in the air?
It certainly does tempt –
I'd be a stronger king than he
Then no life is exempt.

I'd kill my rivals, one by one
And all their children too...!
Was that me talking? Listen, son,
It could be me, or you!

2009
(Inspired by Shakespeare's 'Macbeth', Herod's Massacre of the Innocents and all usurpers and despots).

Seventy-Seventh Birthday

At seventy-seven today – Hurrah!
I'm filled with fresh ambition
To write annoying poems – Hurrah!
With hubris and precision

Pavarotti 'popped his clogs'
Aged seventy-two you know
You can't get rid of me so easy
'On with the Motley' show!

I celebrate my seventy-seventh
Birthday with elation
As in 'the War' we used to say,
'I'm here for the duration!'

2012

When Doubts Ignored

When doubts ignored are crying to our mind –
Like consciences, they will not give us peace
Until we turn and say, 'What's wrong with you?'
And hear them out to give their evidence.
They cry to us for justice – 'Hear our case!
Don't fear it – it's your ally in this cause.
You're wearied with our voice, but fear to hark –
The verdict may demand too much, or take –
Take *everything*.'

No scholar we, and shall we yet presume
Imperfectly equipped, to question truth?
Unthinkable. Oh monstrous proposition!
Dismiss at once, and trouble us no more.

What's this? What bold announcement claims attention?
'Truth, advocate of doubt, begs audience!'
What crazy fancy's this, that truth should come
And stand before us, bid us act the judge?
Dismiss you, wild imaginings, we laugh!

But even as we laugh and turn – it's there,
Silent, cold-eyed, waiting for our stare.

We pause to recollect ourself awhile
'Fore circumstance which so unequal seems.
Now must we question truth, and say to him,
'If you exist at all then do you speak.'

Who says, 'If I exist, reply I do,
The mere concept of order witness be.
You question me. I'll vindicate myself.'

'Well then, what do you here?' again we ask.
Who says, 'I advocate attention to
Those doubts you've long ignored.'
'But where are they?'
'They are behind you.'

We pray Almighty God, He'll 'wait us here,
For we must go, to question even Himself
If He it is that made us minds to think
And let the doubts arise to be resolved.

Then slow, with fear and horror in our hand
We turn, and look with calm, determined eyes –
Look straight upon those monstrous spectral things.

With growing interest and lessened fear
We contemplate their form, their mode, their claims.
And answers come within the weeks and months
And cries for justice trouble not our mind.

1961

At Ladram Bay

Dank sea mist crawls around the rocks
The weird red rocks at Ladram Bay.
I thought the ghosts of yester year
Crept out, then in, to mock the day –
I caught the screams of drowning slaves –
Yes, do you hear them too, my dear?
The fog clings close and smells of graves –
Ghosts of the drowned now shriek and jeer
As we are drawn beneath sad waves
And terror ends the death of fear.

2017

To the Poet Dylan Thomas

An Occupational Hazard

Is it most beautiful and good
To scream that I must die
Or would it yet be nobler to
Look death right in the eye?
For what is death – is it foe or friend?
Is my last breath the awful end
The terror that is nigh?
Perhaps the dreaded cross is hope
As pointing to the sky.

Though Dylan raged against the night
He knew that none survive,
While winter seedlings germinate
And sperm and ovum thrive.

2015

The Pacifist

But who can say 'kill or be killed'
Is it ever justified?
Can he be asked, who died for all,
The gentle crucified?

Though if I see a little child
Held hostage with a gun
Could I stand by, and not prevent
An evil being done
And should I never try to halt
Another crucifixion –

Or is my peaceful protest nothing
But a well-meant fiction?

2009

The Second Coming

He is the coming one
His face is hard like igneous rock
No force can resist his will
Driven with the storm
He advances from the east
His features cold as ice
From the speed of his on-rush.

Cutting through the thin air
He blasts a pathway
With the violence of his passage
Nothing can prevent
The fulfilment of his destiny.

Cold and fierce his eyes
As two stars on a winter night
His lips distorted by the wind
As he hurtles towards his mighty goal.

He is the coming one!
Throughout the centuries and millennia
He was eagerly awaited by all oppressed peoples
And now his time is here.

A shout goes up into the night sky
We know the fulfilment of our dream
He is here, the One who is to bring deliverance
And we are very afraid…!!!

2011

The Phoenix

My parent lived a thousand years
She sang so sweet and long
She sang until her spirit broke
And flames consumed her song.

But from the ashes of her pyre
A new-born phoenix came
She gave me plumage and sweet voice
Her daughter of the flame

I am a lovely phoenix
In red and gold and green
A human in disguise am I
From flames and fire a queen.

2014

Treacle

Treacle is a pretty cat
with treacle-coloured fur
She lives with Steve at SidSoft
though she doesn't often purr.

She frequently sits in the shop
when customers are few
And keeping Helen company
Is nice for Treacle too.

Sometimes she is so mischievous
With startling change of mind
She likes to dash both in and out,
But Steve is very kind,

He acts as doorman for the cat
to open and to close
We feel she likes to do this just
To keep Steve on his toes.

I'm sure some customers like me
pop in to see the cat
When buying things is an excuse
It's nothing more than that!

We know that Treacle likes to view
The art in Sally's shop
In fact she's so intrigued it's true
She always wants to stop,

When Steve and Helen call her name,
no, Treacle will not come,
She hides behind a picture frame,
and thinks it's all good fun.

So what can Sally do to lock
the door and go off home,
With Treacle still in residence?
She can't be left alone.

While all the shops in Church Street close
Just two are open still!
Everyone in Church Street knows
That Treacle roams at will.

She might come home to SidSoft when
Steve and Helen call
Or maybe roam the church yard then
and not come home at all.

And Treacle is so charming,
She has wild-cat genes inside,
As all cats do alarmingly
With independent pride!

2018

Her Hair as Flames

That flicker on the breeze
Forever searching, search the sparkling air
Her golden feet which with angelic ease
Aspire to climb Heaven's holy golden stair
Where myriad flocks of swallows swirl and cry
And never 'light on gilt-edged clouds too rare
Beyond earth's outer limits fly
Enraptured by her burnished haloed hair.
Though clever men will wisely try to hold
And bind her with their deathly earnest lore
May she, more truly wise and yet more bold
Triumphant in strange bliss forever soar.

2015

Night

Night – is it waiting?
Breathes soft and calm
And sees the moon arise
Cool and white

Night – is it waiting?
Sobs, daring not to breathe
Rustling leaves are listening
Through the dark

The moon hangs poised upon a void
Its beams cut sharp as knives
To pierce and shatter fragile air
And search the vacant skies

The moon has slid behind a cloud
Brown earth is still
Rustling leaves are listening, listening –
Courage! Great trees.

1967

When Images

When Images from spirit, soul or mind
Are brought to pain by lumpen barren earth
I look around me and I try to find
Some beauty in the sky of rarer worth.

When churnings on the brutish earthen plane
Abound in broken bodies such as this
I look around me and I try to find
A greater solace and a nobler bliss.

When hurtful eyes betray me as I read
The keener ears detect a sweet employ
I search around me and I gladly find
The human music of a secret joy.

Though guilt or rancour gnaw within man's soul
Their worm shall never yet consume the whole –
Disfigured, scars transform to loveliness
His silent coat worn over battle dress.

2013

Where Are You, My Love

Where are you, my love?
My dear one?
Your voice is vibrant on the air
It is on the wind
It floats and hovers
All around me.
But where are you?
Your voice is lost
On the hills
And over the sea –
Come –
Oh, I know you may not come
But send your dear voice –
May it not come to me on the breezes
Known only to the mists that drift over
the surface of the waves
So I may die in their soft embrace.

2008

Just Once

Your dear sweet mouth touched mine
But that was once upon a time –
A brief encounter would you say?
But long ago and far away.

1966

Peace Not War

Should armaments be forged and sold
To regimes who wage war
Must UK buy their fluid gold
Which makes the climate poor?

Some countries do not want agreement
All they want is war
Their wish is to exterminate
The peoples they abhor.

It never does occur to them
To peacefully engage.
Cain killed his brother Abel
In a fit of jealous rage.

We ask who is the most to blame
If not those foreign powers?
A weapon's made to kill or maim
But could the fault be ours?

Are we too timid to cry out
Against this sort of violence?
Are we complicit with our doubt
Our fear and guilty silence?

So why do Brits sell weaponry
To nations who wage war?
All people are our brothers and
Our sisters, by love's lore.

May God forgive us all we pray,
And may all warfare cease,
May men of power and vision say,
'My brothers, walk in peace!'

2020

Pollution

Pollution has become a curse,
The worst we've ever seen,
Pollution threatens life on Earth
More than Covid 19.

The Covid 19 virus kills
The oldest and the weak,
And those who live in crowded towns
Face prospects that are bleak.

But seas that are polluted by
Our plastics are not good,
They kill the tiny plankton
Which for many fish are food.

The corals are destroyed because
The sea is much too warm,
They need the proper temperature
Or else they cannot spawn.

One cause is carbon dioxide
And some of course we need
But some's enough, and not too much,
Not levels we exceed!

The lovely corals they die out,
Ecology is harmed
And climate change is rampant –
Are our governments alarmed?

What can we do? We can but write
To our MP and press
And use less plastic, even none,
Though none is far the best.

2020

Wealth and Poverty

God is the Father of us all
As we so often pray,
His is the Earth where-on we walk
Not ours to claim our way.

Not ours to desecrate and spoil,
Nor selfishly lay claim
And say 'You are not welcome here'
To homeless in the rain.

We should tend lovingly the Earth –
There always are the poor,
But massive wealth and massive power
Insult those who endure.

2020

A Glass of Beer

I like a glass of beer myself
It does 'Go down a treat'
Especially in company
While folk are on their feet!

The poet Omar Khayyám wrote
'While you live, drink!'
Which might be good advice for some
In moderation, think!

2021

Nature

The worms improve a healthy soil
As do the snails and slugs,
The birds and bees spread pollen so
Nature loves little bugs.

Some farmers use a pesticide
To spray on fields and crops,
Though butterflies and caterpillars
Fertilize the hops!

2021

Song of Mixed Race

We all of us are immigrants
As we already knew
We're Romans, Normans, Vikings and
Some Orangemen a few.

Some have Arabic descent,
And Caribbean others –
Of those some Africans were sent
And sold as slaves, our brothers!

Some are Saxon, some are Jews,
And all are justly proud.
Though deeds were done so shameful
That we confess those aloud.

Then the Windrush scandals loomed
For which we share some blame
In democratic voting doom –
Our blood is red the same!

Our blood is red the same!

2020

Our Angel Now In Heaven

Teresa was my "Sweetie",
She called me "Little Mother"
We joked and laughed so merrily
At one thing and another.

We criticised the T.V. ads,
They only want our money.
The "One Life" is the worst of all,
They cheat with words of honey.

Teresa could be fierce,
Injustice she would fight,
And cruelty would top her list
Of causes to put right.

She always gave the money which
She could to charity,
And running stalls for raising funds
Was a priority.

Such a warm heart Teresa had,
She loved all those we know,
An angel in the heavens now
To bless us here below.

2022

To Teresa

My sweet, my little elfin,
You always are my joy.
Your ashes by the roots of trees
Can never be destroyed.

And nourished by both sun and rain
In trees and hearts you live.
Your love for every creature
Cries in Heaven to forgive.

Forgive a lack of love on earth
Because your love was broad,
From Heaven it streams so bountiful
To all on Earth out-poured.

Your goodness and your courage shone,
Examples to the poor.
Your friendship to the homeless
Was natural and sure.

My sweet, my little elfin,
You always are my joy
You'll always live inside our hearts
Which nothing cannot destroy.

2022

A Ball of Fire

Teresa was a little ball of fire!
She could be fierce as I have said before.
This came from her innate goodness entire
Her love so strong for those she would restore.

She seemed perhaps more gentle and retiring
But her rippling laughter rose upon a word
If unexpected, witty or opposing –
Yet never when her sympathies were stirred!

2022

FRENCH POEMS

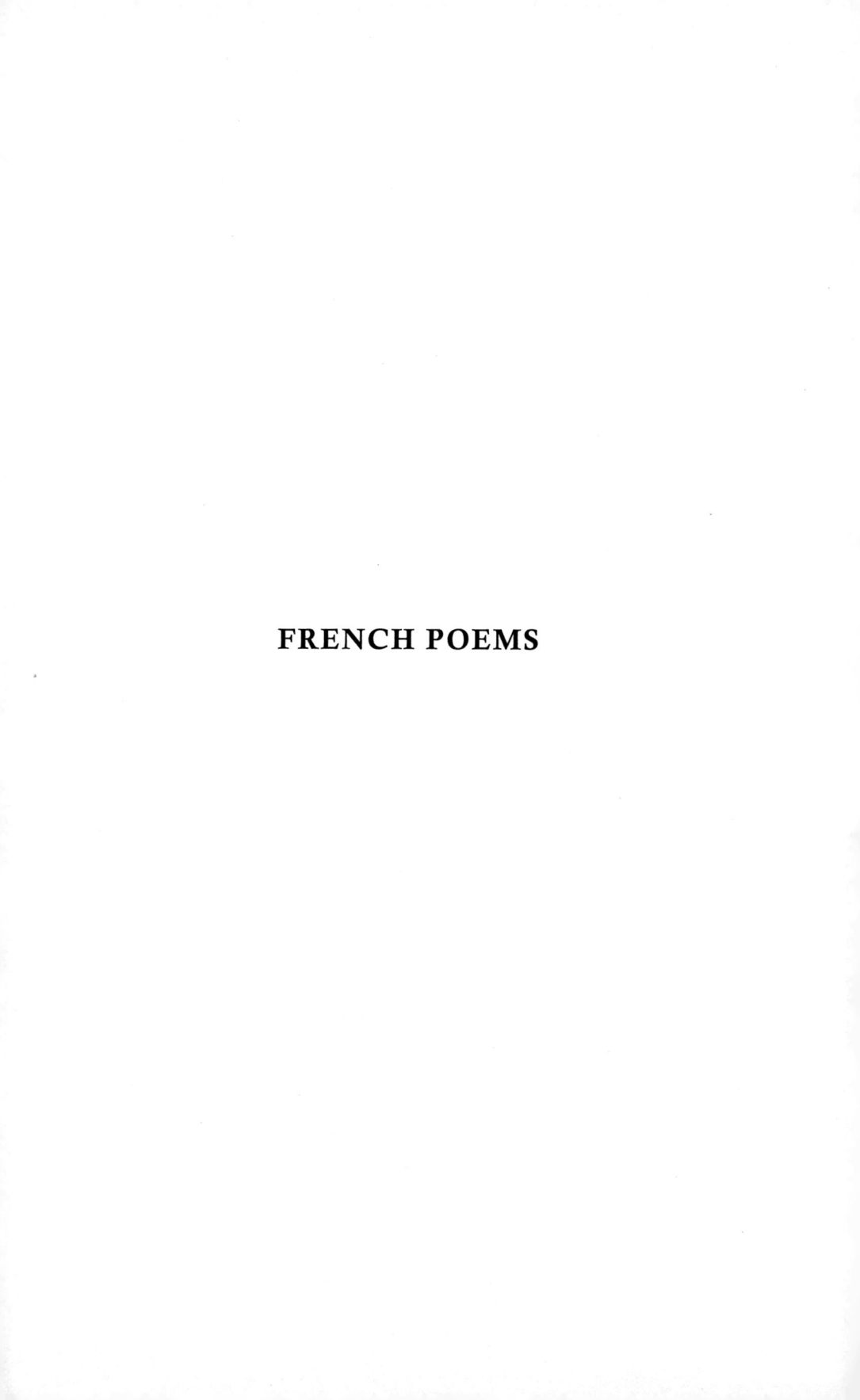

Poème 1

Le vent qui siffle
Courbe les bouleaux blancs
Depuis ton départ
Je l'entends

Encore, encore
J'attends ton pas
Jamais, jamais
Je n'en deviens las

1976

Poem 1

The wind that whistles
Bends the silver birches
Since you went away
I have been hearing it

Always, always
I wait for your step
Never, never
Do I grow tired of waiting.

Poème 2

Elle porte une écharpe rouge
Sales les genoux
Sale le cou
La robe tachée de boue
Elle porte une écharpe rouge

Elle porte une écharpe rouge
Au vent les cheveux
Las les yeux
Ayant perdu leur feu
Elle porte une écharpe rouge

1976

Poem 2

She wears a red scarf
Dirty are her knees
Dirty is her neck
Her dress spotted with dirt
She wears a red scarf

She wears a red scarf
Dishevelled is her hair
Tired are her eyes
Having lost their fire
She wears a red scarf.

Poème 3

Elles volent si haut
Les hirondelles
Comme les nuages
Prés du ciel
Comme les étoiles
Et aussi belles
J'aime tant toujours
Les hirondelles!

1976

Poem 3

They fly so high
The swallows
Like the clouds
Close to the heavens
Like the stars
And quite as beautiful
I always love
The swallows!

Poème 4

Je veux t'envelopper, chéri
En douceur et des soins!
J'ai encore mal d'amour chéri
Ne m'oublies pas de loin!

1998

Poem 4

I want to wrap you, darling
In sweetness and attentions!
I am still sick with love darling
Don't forget me from so far away!

Poème 5

Quelle pauvre mie d'amour, chéri
Que tu me donnes, tu sais!
Les larmes s'écoulantes à la terre
Ne m'aimes-tu à jamais?

J'attends, j'attends que tu viennes-
Tu reviens de loin?
Veux-tu me serrer dans les bras
Prés de ton coeur enfin!

1998

Poem 5

What a poor crumb of love my darling
You give to me, you know!
The tears trickling to the ground
Don't you love me anymore?

I wait, I wait for you to come –
Are you coming from far away?
Will you clasp me in your arms
Close to your heart at last!

Poème 6

Ne sais-tu pas la verité?
Crois-tu, donc que je joue?
Les lettres, les larmes, les poèmes, même,
Viennent de moi non plus?

Que puis-je dire enfin, chéri?
Je dois jurer encore
Que tous les mots sont les miens –
Mais sais-tu qui t'adore?

1998

Poem 6

Do you not know the truth?
Do you believe then, that I am only playing?
The letters, the tears, even the poems,
Don't come from me?

What can I say then, darling?
I must swear once again
That all the words are my very own –
But do you know who adores you?

Poème 7

On t'offre en timidité
 Le billet doux du coeur
Mais si tu le refuses encore
Elle mourrait en douleur

Puis qui dise doucement au vent
Que tu me manques, mon cher?
Même je vais mourrir lentement
Mon amour dans la terre.

Joyeuse la terre! déjà la vie!
Le beauté de la rose!
Enivrée du parfum suis-je
Et j'en espére toutes choses!

Partout les mains! Partout la bouche!
Le sens soi-même en feu!
Il faut se taire en silence, donc,
L'orage tumultueux!

Mais tous n'existe sauf dans mes rêves
Mon lit soit solitaire
Je meurs de tristesse, le sais-tu
Et tu me manques, mon cher!

Que tu me cherches! Que tu me trouves!
Peutêtre tu viennes?
Mon âme s'est relevée enfin
Que je sois la tienne!

1998

Poem 7

Someone is shyly offering you
The love letter of her heart
But if you still refuse it
She will die of sorrow.

Then, who will say softly to the wind,
'I miss you, my darling?'
But I shall die slowly
My love within the earth.

Joyful, the earth! Already, life!
The beauty of the rose!
Inebriated by perfume am I
And I am filled with hope!

Everywhere, your hands! Everywhere, your mouth!
The sense itself on fire!
One must keep silence, then –
The storm rages.

But all this exists only in my dreams
My bed is a lonely one
I am dying of sadness, you know –
And I miss you, my darling!

But if you should seek me, would you find me?
Perhaps you will come?
My spirits are lifted at last
Because I might yet be yours!

1998

STORIES

A Coroner's Verdict

'No, it is very peculiar,' I replied to the Coroner's question, 'I think I must have dreamed it.'

'I am not interested in dreams,' said the Coroner. 'In this Court we investigate facts. You say you saw your Aunt Betina go into her husband's study while he was preparing his sermon for the next Sunday. Tell the Court what happened then, Roberta.'

'Well, Aunt Betina did not close the door, and I heard her grumbling to Uncle Timothy that he had left the lamp on in the sitting room. I was curious, so I stepped through the doorway into his study. My long silk dress rustled around my ankles, but neither Betina nor Timothy was aware of me.

'Timothy told his wife not to interrupt his work with trivial matters. They argued, their voices rose, but neither of them was listening to the other. Timothy stood up. He was shaking. I sensed that after years of being nagged at by his wife, his irritation had reached a climax. He picked up a paper weight from his desk top and hit Betina on her forehead. She fell to the floor, crumpled amongst her Victorian clothes. Timothy's expression changed from anger to horror when he realised what he had done.

'I screamed. It was then that Timothy noticed me. He dropped the paper weight and flopped into his chair. He looked really ill. I asked him if he would like some water or brandy. 'A large brandy, please, Roberta,' he said hoarsely, and added, 'You should have one, too.' There was a decanter on a side table, so I poured two glasses. The brandy made us feel much better.

'The question in both our minds was what to do next. I suggested burying Aunt Betina's body in the garden. We waited until it was quite dark, then set to work. We spoke in whispers, and agreed to invent a story about Betina's having gone away to stay with a sick relative.

'Afterwards we were exhausted. I advised Uncle to go to bed. I went home to my flat in the village and tumbled onto my own bed. I slept immediately, still wearing my long silk dress.'

At this point the Coroner stopped me, and told me that I could stand down. She said, 'The skeleton of a woman dressed in Victorian clothes has been found buried in the parsonage garden of St. Cuthbert's church. The skeleton has a deep depression in the left temple. The pathologist's report states that death occurred approximately one hundred and fifty years ago, probably due to a blow from a heavy object. The woman, whoever she was, was murdered by a person unknown, long before you were born, Roberta Stevens.'

Suddenly my alarm clock rang. I found myself sitting on the side of my bed, dressed in the jumper and skirt I had worn the previous day. There was no Court room and no Coroner. I took a quick shower and a change of clothes, then after a cup of coffee I hurried to catch the bus to the supermarket where I work. I was so busy at the till all day that I forgot about my dream – or experience – of the night before. But when I got back to my flat after work, I took the old photo album from my bookcase, and leafing through it I found what I was looking for – a discoloured photograph of Uncle Timothy and Aunt Betina in their Victorian clothes, and a younger woman seated between them wearing a long silk dress!

2016

What If

What if she hadn't turned around as she reached the door! My heart skipped a beat, quite literally. So did she care after all? But in seconds she was gone. What did it mean, that glance of hers, that parting gesture? Was it merely curiosity, to see how I was bearing the break-up of our marriage? Or something more? Soon the kids would be home from school. Neither of them had any inkling that Janice was leaving us. It would be a shock to them, and how was I going to tell them?

I knew that Janice had not been happy recently. Often she'd stayed out until the small hours, long after midnight. Had she found someone else? She never told me where she had been or with whom. Plainly something was very wrong.

I sat at the kitchen table, miserable and pondering. I forgot about the time, and was startled when the front door opened and the kids rushed in. They dumped their satchels on the floor in the hall and burst into the kitchen where I was still sitting immobile.

'Mummy, Mummy what's for tea?' they shouted and, 'Where's Janice, is she in?'

Then I recalled the glance that Janice had given me before she went out through the door. So I replied, 'No, Janice is not in, but I think she will come back, my dears,' and I began to prepare the tea.

2014

The Underworn Underwear

This is a story about some underwear which never gets worn, hence the title.

The army distributed a wonderful new issue of old stock previous generation underpants.

The soldiers' wives and girlfriends were dismayed. They whispered conspiratorially, 'You can't wear those, someone might see them!'

Consequently, the soldiers were demoralised and lost the will to fight.

Their superior officers decided to offer a pair of the underpants to the prisoner who was to be shot at dawn. They said, 'The prisoner will be delighted to die wearing some smart underpants!' But when the underpants were shown to him the prisoner shrieked, 'I shall die honourably, wearing the underpants of my fatherland! I refuse to die wearing the underpants of some tin pot nation!'

So the army donated the underpants to the troop leader of the local scouts, who gave them to the parents. The boys' mothers were delighted, and presented them to their sons for Christmas. The boys sniggered, and in a burst of generosity they donated the underpants to 'the poor'. 'The poor' also sniggered, and put the offending garments into a charity shop collection bag.

The charity shop was grateful, and placed the underwear on display. But the public was bored, and the charity shop went into receivership. The Official Receiver sent everything to a church jumble sale, where the customers politely ignored the underpants. All the leftovers from the jumble sale were collected by a 'rag and bone man' at great expense to the church, and being sorted, the underpants were turned into high quality writing paper thus saving trees.

The writing paper was used by Buckingham Palace to invite the soldiers to be decorated with medals for bravery, the soldiers to whom the underworn underwear had originally been issued. And this concludes my story.

I do like a happy ending!

2003

The Underwired Bra

Sequel to 'The Underworn Underwear'

A pretty little lacy black bra was exposed (sorry, displayed) on a model in the window of a shop.

It was priced at £50 reduced to £5 because one hook was missing from the back, thus leaving only one hook to fasten it.

A young lady named Christina was holding a party for her 16th birthday, so Mum and Dad obligingly went to the cinema for the evening.

Christina's boyfriend, Justin, noticed the beautiful black bra in the window of the shop and, having a 'fiver' in his pocket, courtesy of his dad, you've guessed it, he sidled into the shop and stammered that he wished to purchase the said article. The bra was handed to Justin in a posh little carrier bag, and he sidled back out of the shop, trying not to look obvious, with the item in its posh bag sticking half in and half out of his anorak pocket.

As Justin slunk along the road, some rude little boys barged up against him and yanked poor Justin's gift out of his pocket and ran away with it shouting in glee.

However, it so happened that a police car came around the corner of the street, and the miscreants guiltily slung the bag with its contents on top of a passing van. The van was travelling at high speed, escaping from the scene of a bank robbery, and the bag with the underwired little bra slid off the roof of the van as it sped along with the police car in pursuit.

The police, surmising (correctly as it happened) that the bag contained stolen goods, stopped their car to retrieve the item. On discovering the little bra together with the till receipt, they returned them to the shop. The shop assistant remembered Justin, and because she knew his mother, she telephoned that lady.

Poor Justin had a lot of explaining to do.

The moral of this story is: Never buy a bra with only one hook because if it breaks, there is no fail-safe mechanism!

2009

Thirteen Minutes Past One

I am not usually superstitious and I don't believe in any paranormal activity at all but then last week on the day the clocks went back, our family was up very late as usual.

We were watching television, that is Grandma, my brother Henry and our sister Anne, and myself Marjorie. Nothing remarkable in that, but Henry suddenly noticed the old wind-up clock on the mantelpiece said the time was one o'clock. He jumped off the sofa and turned the hands back to midnight. We were all a bit 'huffy' because the activity distracted our attention from the murder mystery on the television. But we continued watching. Anne yawned. Grandma nodded off to sleep for a few minutes. The old clock went on ticking.

The television drama became creepier, and we sat glued to the box. The granny in the film had grown tired of a life with grandad's unpleasant habits and constant grumbling. I yawned, and Grandma fidgeted. Although we all felt sleepy, we wanted to see the end of the story. The plot continued with the old grandad falling into a drunken sleep. What happened next in the film gave us all a shock – the evil old woman took a cushion from the settee and smothered her husband! She glanced up at their clock-the time was thirteen minutes past one. She gave a malicious grin.

Suddenly our clock stopped ticking, and Grandma gave a horrible scream! She jumped up and pointed to the clock – it had stopped at thirteen minutes past one! Then she shuddered and collapsed.

Henry said to me, 'You must try to revive her, Marjorie, while I call for an ambulance.' I did the best I could, and I went in the ambulance with Grandma. But she died before we reached the hospital.

After Grandma's funeral, Henry tried to get our old clock working again but without success. The hands always point to thirteen minutes past one!

2014

Unfinished Business

We first met by the bridge. He could not have been more than fourteen. I noticed him looking into the water, his hands clutching the stone wall. I was intrigued. It was late, nearly 11 o'clock. Why wasn't he at home in bed asleep? I had come out of the pub, where I'd been drinking with my mates, and I wanted to sober up before going home to Sally, my wife. The kids must have been put to bed long ago. I decided to say something. 'Waiting for someone?' I asked. The boy nodded. 'Have you got somewhere to go to?' I carried on.

At last he spoke. 'Yes, I've got a squat. The tenants moved out a couple of weeks back. There's David. And Brian. This chap I ran into said he'd meet me here. Have you got any money?' he asked, which quite took me by surprise.

'Well, what do you want it for?' I stammered. Then I saw the flick-knife, as he drew it from his pocket. I thought quickly. 'I haven't got much,' I carried on, 'I spent most of it at the pub.' Looking again at the knife, I added, 'I think I've got a tenner.'

'Okay, that'll do. It's for the dealer.' I took the tenner from my pocket. He grabbed it and ran away.

'See you here same time tomorrow!' I called to him. He waved to me, my tenner in his hand.

2015

Funny Face Betty

Betty Anderson was six years old today. Her birthday party had been fun, several of her class-mates from St. Anne's School came, and Dad hired a man to do conjuring tricks and tell stories. The party was held at Grandad and Grandma's house because it was large. Betty's Aunt Hilary was there of course, she was her mum's sister, and Hilary stayed to help Grandma to tidy up after the guests had gone. Hilary had nearly completed training as a general nurse at Middlesex Hospital. Betty loved her, and they spent as much time together as they could when Hilary was off duty and Betty was not at school.

Now the Andersons were travelling along the North Circular Road to their London home, Dad and Mum in the front of the car, and Betty on the rear seat with one of her friends, Veronica, who was coming to spend the rest of the weekend with Betty. Both little girls were tired after the party and fell asleep.

Dad put on the radio softly. It was 7 o'clock, in January, quite dark except for the street lights and the head lamps of the cars. The traffic was heavy, and Dad drove slowly and carefully. He paid attention to the news – there was a warning of black ice on some of the roads in the South East. At a junction, Dad turned off the North Circular Road. They were nearly home.

Then suddenly a terrible thing occurred – their car skidded on a large patch of black ice! Dad at the steering wheel tried desperately to regain control of the vehicle, but it spun round and went headlong into a concrete wall. It stopped; the front of the car severely smashed. Several cars skidded and stopped too, but the Andersons' car suffered the most damage. Some one used a mobile phone to call for an ambulance and the police.

Being in the front of the car, Mr. and Mrs. Anderson's injuries were the most critical. The ambulance crew tried to save their lives, but despite all their efforts, on arrival at hospital the Andersons were pronounced dead.

Little Betty was given a quiet room, her face had been badly cut by glass. Veronica was treated for shock but otherwise she was unhurt. Her parents came to take her home as soon as they could.

Betty's grandad and grandma came, but they were so distraught at the deaths of their daughter and their son-in-law that they willingly accepted Hilary's offer to break the appalling news to Betty.

Betty's parents were young when they married, hardly nineteen. Of course they should have finished their education, but young love prevailed, and being Catholic they took their parents' advice and were married in church. That was seven years ago, and Hilary was a year older than her sister, Betty's mother.

Now, after the car crash, Hilary made all the funeral arrangements. She obtained some compassionate leave from her nursing duties. It was of course a Catholic funeral.

Betty was not told about her parents' funeral, the fact that they were dead was more than enough for the child to absorb. When a bed became available at Great Ormond Street Children's Hospital, Betty was transferred to a pretty room there. Hilary visited as often as she could.

Betty's plastic surgery to her face took many weeks of operations.

Grandad and Grandma visited too but less often, they were badly shaken by the terrible events and unable to empathise with the physically and emotionally traumatised little orphan.

Hilary never argued with her family about the Catholic Church, but she resolved that one day when she felt ready she would leave. Sometimes she asked herself whether she was being hypocritical by conforming outwardly, but then reminded herself that her life of service as a trainee General Nurse was not blameworthy by any standard. Her final exams were due soon, and since she was a conscientious student most of the studies were now behind her and she found more time to visit Betty at Great Ormond Street.

During the intervals between further operations for plastic surgery, Betty was allowed to return to St. Anne's Catholic Junior School. She kept quiet about the teasing in the playground as children usually do in such circumstances. And her grandparents ignored the little girl's emotional scarring, choosing to believe as people often do, that if you pretend everything is all right, then it will be.

Hilary sat her final exams, and now she was a Registered General Nurse with a career before her. The Middlesex Hospital offered her a post as a staff nurse, but on reflection she decided to take some leave and then apply for a job outside the capital city, somewhere she could rent a flat.

Hilary and Betty had always been close, but due to the family arrangements and Hilary's hours as a trainee nurse, they had not spent much time together. Visiting hours at Great Ormond Street enabled them to form a deep friendship. Hilary was sensitive to the troubled little girl. She applied for a position as a staff nurse at the Royal Sussex County Hospital in Brighton and was accepted for the post.

Hilary loved being near the seaside. She found a flat to rent over a shop in a side street. At the back of her mind she had a plan. Her plan was to bring her little niece to Brighton to live with her. She knew that Betty would never be happy with her grandparents in London. So now she bought some good quality second hand furniture and decorated the flat during the next few months. Her bank balance was low by this time, but she managed to secure a loan, and her new job started in June. She was ready.

An invitation to visit Brighton by train one Sunday in July was accepted, and Grandpa and Grandma brought Betty to have tea with Hilary. A pretty bedroom was shown to Betty, nicely furnished with dolls and a dolls' house, and colourful curtains and bed covers.

While little Betty was occupied with the dolls and a picture book, Hilary asked the grandparents to consider allowing her to bring up their grandchild and enrol her at a school in Brighton. After some discussion it was agreed, and Betty's grandparents said she should attend St. John's Junior School, and that she could stay with them in the school holidays. When this news was told to Betty she was excited and pleased, and ran to Hilary to hug her, then she hugged both of her grandparents.

At St. John's School, Hilary and Betty's grandparents met the Sister Superior who was kind and understood. Later, Hilary reflected how glad she was that she had never disclosed her own feelings about religion.

And so it was that in September, Betty came to live with Hilary, and started attending her new school.

At first Betty's classmates stared at the little girl with the scarred cheeks and nose. But she was a clever child and turned her appearance to her advantage, pulling comical grimaces and making the children laugh. Soon they found a nickname for her, "Funny Face Betty". She did not mind at all, and it was not long before she became the most popular girl in the school.

Hilary said morning and evening prayers with the child and took her to Mass on Sundays. When the time came for her First Communion, then Confirmation, Grandpa and Grandma took a train from London and spent the day with Betty and Hilary.

Because Hilary's work was at the outpatients department in the hospital, she was able to keep regular hours. However, a difficulty arose when Betty was approaching secondary school age as her grandparents wanted her to continue in Catholic education. Hilary gave this much thought.

Eventually it was agreed that Betty would attend the comprehensive school and receive religious instruction in a weekly class.

At her new school the teachers addressed her as Betty, but she introduced herself to her class mates as 'Funny Face Betty' which instantly brought her many friends.

And wherever she went, people loved Betty for her warm smile and irrepressible sense of humour.

2008

The Curtain Twitch'd

It was the summer of 2010. Sarah had been invited by her friend Elizabeth to spend three weeks at the cottage in Plymouth where she lived with her grandmother.

Sarah's parental home was in a village not far from Maidenhead in Berkshire, and the girls had met each other at several animal rights rallies in Bristol. Sarah had never been further west than Bristol, so she was looking forward to seeing more of the West Country.

The girls were awaiting their A-level results. Sarah wanted to read Modern History at Liverpool, and Elizabeth was hoping to study English literature at Southampton.

This afternoon they had attended the animal rights meeting, and when it was over they went to Bristol Temple Meads station together to take a train for Plymouth, changing at Torquay. On the train, Elizabeth became engrossed in a women's magazine, and Sarah was left alone with her thoughts.

Sarah recalled Elizabeth telling her that when she was a baby her mother had walked out, leaving her to be brought up by Gran, as she called her grandmother.

There were times when Sarah was not entirely sure that Elizabeth was truthful, she reflected, although she had never been able to think of a specific incident that would confirm it beyond doubt. So now she laid aside any feelings of uneasiness for the sake of their friendship, and resolved to enjoy her holiday, watching the countryside they were passing through from the window of the train. Eventually they reached Torquay, and changed to a train bound for Plymouth.

On arrival at Plymouth, a short bus ride brought them to Grandmother's house. Sarah was surprised at the tiny road with tiny houses close together, but she said nothing, remembering this was Elizabeth's home.

Elizabeth rang the doorbell of no.18 Trent Street, then she fumbled for her key and entered the little house, with Sarah behind her. No-one was at home; Elizabeth said that Gran must be out at the shops.

Sarah was dismayed at how small and dingy the house was. She felt a chill in the air, it seemed somehow spooky. They were standing in a tiny passage, with the steep narrow staircase immediately opposite the front door.

Unexpectedly Elizabeth spoke. She said, 'This is the kitchen, here on the left. I'll put the kettle on. If you'd like to go into the lounge, it's that door over there. Do make yourself comfortable, I shan't be long. And Gran will be back soon.' Sarah obeyed, although she nearly tripped over their rucksacks in the narrow dark passageway.

The lounge was crowded, with a two-seater sofa, three chairs, a dining table, and a shelf with a few books. Sarah took down an old photograph album. The faded faces seemed to stare right through her, almost as though they were looking at someone behind her. She shut the album hurriedly and replaced it on the shelf, trying not to shudder.

Soon the door was opened, and Elizabeth brought in two mugs of tea. 'It's cold in here,' she remarked. 'I'll put the fire on.' She switched on an ancient electrical fire, and almost instantly the room became more cheerful.

The two girls had nearly finished drinking their tea, when a key was turned in the front door lock, and a bird-like figure came in. She nearly tripped over the two rucksacks. Then she spoke. Her voice was high and screeching, as she complained about the luggage. Then she noticed Sarah, who had come into the passage to greet her. The old lady immediately screamed "Sex and drugs! Sex and drugs! That's all you young girls think about nowadays!" She went into the kitchen, still grumbling in a thin high voice, and unpacked her shopping. "You needn't imagine you'll get well fed here!" She told Sarah, "Fish fingers and oven chips. Like it or leave it!" Sarah tried to reply, "That will be lovely!" but the old lady wasn't listening.

Sleeping arrangements too were Spartan. Upstairs there was one small double bedroom, where Gran and Elizabeth each had a single bed, the second bedroom having been made into a bathroom.

Sarah found that she was expected to sleep on the two-seater sofa in the lounge. She thought with dismay on the three weeks looming ahead and made up her mind to find an excuse to shorten her visit. After an evening meal consisting of the fish fingers and oven chips, Sarah spent an uneasy night on the sofa, unable to stretch out her legs and cramped into foetal position.

The following morning, all three people had their breakfast in the kitchen. Elizabeth ate her coco-pops standing up, as there were only two chairs.

Gran kept up a one-sided conversation telling Sarah over and over again that Elizabeth wanted her to die so that she could inherit the house. Between her sentences she shrieked "Sex and drugs! Sex and drugs!" Somewhat like a mantra, Sarah thought.

After breakfast the girls decided to take a bus into the town centre, to "do the charity shops" as there were several in Plymouth. Sarah was glad to get away from the spooky little house for a few hours. The girls spent the whole day out, and had a snack in a café. Sarah bought two pretty tee-shirts, and Elizabeth found an old book of horror stories on a shelf, and bought it for a few pence. At 4 o'clock the charity shops closed, and it began to rain. The girls caught a bus back to 18 Trent Street, and when they got indoors their clothes were damp.

Gran was at home, shrieking and grumbling as usual. "I suppose you'll be wanting something to eat! Well, it'll be fish fingers and oven chips again. Like it or leave it!" Sarah tried to thank her, but she could not make herself heard, as Gran seemed never to pause to take a breath.

Elizabeth went upstairs to the bedroom, to change into some dry clothes. Fortunately Sarah was not so damp, because her jacket was waterproof. However, she needed some dry footwear, so she went into the lounge, took off her trainers and pushed her feet into soft slippers. In the meantime, Gran had followed Elizabeth upstairs and gone into the bathroom.

Then Sarah heard Gran come out of the bathroom and close the door. Suddenly, there was a terrifying scream which reverberated throughout the entire house and could be heard outside in the street. The terrible scream was succeeded by a series of thumps. Fearfully Sarah ran to the door of the lounge and opened it. In the dim passageway Gran lay at the foot of the stairs, with her head at an odd angle.

Horrified, Sarah glanced up, and saw Elizabeth standing on the tiny landing between the bathroom and bedroom doors. "Is she dead?" asked Elizabeth, in a strained harsh voice. Sarah said "I think so. We'd best call an ambulance."

There was no telephone in the house, but Sarah had her mobile phone in her rucksack, and she contacted the ambulance service. While she was doing this, a concerned neighbour rang the doorbell, and wanted to know if everything was all right, having heard the scream. 'No,' said Sarah, 'Gran has had a fall, but the ambulance is on its way.'

'Is there anything I can do?' asked the lady kindly. 'I am Doreen James, I live at no.17, across the road.'

'Not at the moment, but maybe later,' Sarah replied. 'Thank you, Mrs James.'

Elizabeth sat in the kitchen, saying nothing. She is suffering from shock, thought Sarah.

It was not long before the ambulance came. The girls were allowed to accompany Gran to the hospital. But she was pronounced dead on arrival.

During the days that followed, Sarah took charge of everything necessary, while Elizabeth sat in the kitchen, scarcely speaking unless she were asked a direct question. Sarah changed the sheets on Gran's bed and slept there herself, at least now she could stretch out comfortably, and she resolved to stay on as long as she could, if Elizabeth needed her.

Mrs James was very supportive. She told Sarah how to find the laundrette and the bank as well as helping to sort out the matters in connection with the doctor, the solicitor, and the police. Elizabeth still seemed to be in shock, and let Sarah do everything.

Sometimes Sarah went across the street to no.17 for coffee with Doreen in her kitchen. Doreen's husband John had died of a heart attack three years previously. Their daughter was married, with two children, and lived in New Zealand. John was a builder, and although their house was no larger than no. 18, it was nicely decorated, the kitchen in pale apricot, with curtains in a floral design.

One day Doreen told Sarah the story of Elizabeth's background. Elizabeth's mother, Alice, had never said who the father was. When she was eight months pregnant with Elizabeth, a tragedy occurred in their family. Elizabeth's grandfather had fallen down the steep staircase, breaking his neck.

Doreen said that when Grandfather had the fall, John noticed a white face at the bedroom window of no. 18 and the curtain twitched. Whether or not he was pushed was never established. Probably as a result of the shock, Alice gave birth to Elizabeth a month prematurely. A few weeks later she left no. 18 Trent Street. Maybe she went abroad, but she was never traced. 'That is why Elizabeth was brought up by Gran,' Doreen explained.

But now there were to be legal proceedings and correspondence arrived from the Coroner's office with regard to an inquest. On the day of the inquest, Doreen shared a taxi with Elizabeth and Sarah. At the inquest, the Coroner returned an open verdict. The old lady could not have been pushed – could she?

Sarah had to swear under oath that the only other person upstairs was Elizabeth. Mrs James swore under oath that at exactly the same moment as she heard the scream, a white face appeared at the bedroom window and the curtain twitched.

So did anyone push Gran? And whose was the face at the window when Gran screamed and the curtain twitched?

2009

The Break with Tradition

'Today is going to be exciting!' Helena Watson reflected as she wandered amongst the sets in the 'Small Gardens Competition'. One of the exhibits was her own.

It was early morning, and sunny, which would please the exhibitors and visitors alike and would put the judges into a good mood. This year the competition was different, the theme being 'Innovation'. Every year until now the gardens had been traditional, but Sir Justin Halberton, who had organised it annually for fifty-four of his eighty years, had gone the way of all flesh, and his granddaughter Amelia Halberton wanted to make a break with tradition. It was an escape from the 'fuddy duddy' habits which Sir Justin imposed on his family. He was terrified by washing machines, and believed foreign foods to be the cause of war. Holidays were taken only in Scunthorpe, anywhere else the air was certain to be injurious to health.

So Amelia decided to be creative this year with a theme 'Innovation'. The break with tradition.

Amelia's mother had died giving birth to her, and now her father was suffering from a brain tumour. So she had power of attorney to manage the mansion and large estate in Dorset until such time as she would inherit outright. She was age 40 this year, and had studied the classics at college, then a course in estate management which she knew a lot about already.

Twice she had been engaged. The first time she was studying in London and living with her boyfriend David. After David proposed, she discovered he was paying maintenance for a six-year-old son from a previous relationship. Marrying Amelia would have seemed a way out of his financial difficulties. Amelia confronted him and they had a terrible row. David assured Amelia that he had intended to tell her when he found the right moment! But she was not in the mood to listen to excuses.

Two years after splitting up with David, she met Charles. Charles was working for Ph.D. at Cambridge researching into sugar substitutes. Charles was often absorbed in his research, and not exactly practical in terms of day-to-day life. They had been dating for three years and Amelia felt the relationship was not going anywhere. So on one of their country walks, Amelia gently brought up the question of marrying. Charles was genuinely surprised, but said he thought it was a 'good idea'. He never mentioned it subsequently however, and Amelia felt he had forgotten. She stopped contacting him, and he was so absorbed in his research that he didn't notice! She returned home to the Halberton Estate.

It was 6 o'clock on the morning of a Sunday in June, the day for judging the winner of the 'Small Gardens Competition'. Amelia was out of bed and showered and dressed, and after some coffee and a croissant, she stepped from the house, pulling a shawl around her shoulders. The air felt cool, but she knew it would get hot later in the day.

The site of the 'Small Gardens Competition' was on the estate within twenty minutes' walking distance along a metalled road, and Amelia strode out confidently. She had put a lot of energy into organising the event, and set aside some money from her estate accounts to help exhibitors on low incomes. Making a garden exhibit, even a small one, can be costly. Each year the trustees presented a silver-plated cup to the winner. This year the judges were to be Duncan and Anne Gooding from the National Trust; they had offered their services free in the hope of enrolling some new members.

As Amelia walked along the road she became warm, and slipped off her shawl and carried it on her arm. When she reached the site, vans were coming and going, and people busily putting finishing touches to their garden exhibits. Each garden was separated from the next by one yard, and altogether there were twelve gardens, each 8 ft by 8 ft in size. Each was walled or fenced and had an entrance. Several hundred yards away was a row of poplars which acted as a wind-break, and the whole of the site was sheltered.

Amelia was delighted at the activity and to see everyone so keen. They had all been working hard for months, and those who were employed in daily jobs devoted every minute they could spare to the task.

She walked amongst the gardens, trying not to get in people's way, and greeting those whom she knew.

One particular garden caused her to stop, startled, and take in a deep breath. This was Helena's. It flamed with every colour imaginable!

Helena's parents had come to the UK from Jamaica in search of work in the early 1960's. Helena was born in Cricklewood, London, and after taking her A-levels at the local comprehensive school, she had trained as a nursery nurse. Helena loved children; she also loved gardens and gardening, and watched the gardening programmes on television. As a qualified nursery nurse she was now working at a "live-in" job in Dorchester, Dorset. Her employers were happy for Helena to care of their garden in her spare time, and paid her for this. Seeing the "Small Gardens Competition" advertised locally, Helena thought she would like to enter. The title of the competition attracted her, "Innovation". There was plenty of scope in that, she decided.

The advertisement said that would-be entrants could apply for a grant. Helena took the opportunity. When a letter came in reply to her application, she was excited to find the Trustees were offering her the loan of a van, and some vouchers.

Now she could plan her garden.

Helena was resourceful. She always bought her fruit and vegetables at a local Caribbean shop. She began to save seeds and roots and cuttings. Some she grew on the windowsill of her room, and others under glass panes in a part of the nursery garden which was shut off from the main section. She took the van to the recycling centre, making several trips to carry fencing. One of the exhibitors, Adrian, noticed Helena hard at work, and he realised she could not manage everything alone, so he offered to help. The fence really did need a strong back and arm.

Once the fence was installed, Helena primed and painted it in bright colours, green, black and gold, the colours of the Jamaican flag. She and Adrian dug over the earth. At last she was ready to plant her fruit and vegetables.

When Amelia noticed Helena's garden on the morning of the competition, she hurried back to the house in time to greet the judges, Duncan and Anne. She said nothing of what she had seen. After coffee and biscuits, Amelia drove the judges in her car to the site of the competition.

There was no difficulty in deciding who had won first prize! Helena's orange and lemon trees formed a dark green backdrop against the green, black and gold fence. Red Scotch bullet peppers contrasted with the dark brown of the soil. In yellow, red and green, some peppers shone amongst the coriander, the ginger, and the orange of squashes and the yellow of melons. Sweet potatoes, chillies, and the small white flowers of garlic were abundant.

Duncan and Anne gazed in astonishment and were silent for several minutes. The chairman of the trustees presented Helena with the silver cup. There was enthusiastic applause, and she introduced Adrian, without whose help she would not have succeeded.

Amelia was delighted. After some short speeches she invited everyone back to the house for a buffet lunch. Several friendships were formed on that day.

If anyone happened to be in the parish churchyard, they might have imagined the earth move slightly in one corner plot, as Sir Justin Halberton turned in his grave murmuring, 'Tradition…tradition…no break…tradition…'

But Amelia did not hear.

2011

Confession

'You've been in there quite some time.' The voice was soft. 'Are you looking for anything in particular?' I realised he was just at the other side of the door. I felt suddenly chilled.

I hadn't heard anyone approaching. But I knew it was our Parish Priest, Father Augustine. He opened the door and stared at me inquiringly. I felt as though I had been caught cheating in an exam. I couldn't tell him the truth, could I? That all the time he was reading his breviary in the church, I had been searching for the communion wine in the vestry!

I was 48 years of age last Thursday, and I have cirrhosis of the liver. I had been attending Alcoholics Anonymous regularly, but on my birthday last week my wife, Sarah, left me, taking our son with her. Thomas is ten, the joy of my life, and the reason I'd joined AA.

Now I had to give Father Augustine an answer. So I replied facetiously.

'Yes, Father. I've been looking at your books. Have you anything on the Confessions of Saint Augustine?'

I'd never liked our Parish Priest, he is a creepy sort of person, always wearing soft shoes and speaking in a soft silky fashion.

So I was startled by his saying, 'It seems you have something you want to confess, my son. I'll get ready to hear your confession. Come out and join me in ten minutes. That will give us both time to prepare.'

This really did put me in a difficult position, I had only ten minutes in which to act. I am not a person to panic, but that evening and moment I came close to it.

I soon found the communion wine, and slipped the bottle into the deep pocket of my coat. I took off my shoes and held them in my hand, then leaving the vestry door ajar, I went quietly out of the church.

Once outside, I put my shoes on, and ran to catch the bus to go home. I caught a bus easily, and found a seat, but it was rush hour and the traffic was slow. It gave me time to reflect.

My last confession was such a long time ago that I couldn't recall it. My drinking had ruined my marriage and my health, and lost me the job which I'd enjoyed as a journalist for a national daily newspaper. I thought, When I get back to the empty house, I'll write a suicide note for Sarah, and end my wretched life.

When I reached home, I went to my study and switched on the light. I sat at my desk and pulled a sheet of paper towards me, and took a pen to begin writing. Then I realised I hadn't opened the bottle of wine. I thought of the priest who was waiting in the church to hear my confession. Suddenly I knew that God was waiting for me! I felt overcome with joy, and began writing – not a suicide note but the story of my life and my sudden decision to really give up the drink, and to use the time I had left to do charitable work of some sort. It would have to be humble work, due to my history of alcohol abuse; in fact, I'd be grateful to anyone who would take on a reformed addict. And I need help. Perhaps in time Sarah will know how hard I'm trying, and let me see Thomas occasionally.

The following day I returned the bottle of altar wine to Father Augustine, and asked him to hear my confession.

2016

Message in a Bottle

When the tide is out and the sun is shining, it is a joy to paddle in the shallows at Sidmouth. My preferred spot is beside the rock islands. You can approach by the flight of steps from the under-cliff walkway near Jacob's Ladder. The steps lead onto beautiful soft sand, and the cool shallow sea is enticing.

On one such occasion last summer, I took off my sandals at the bottom of the steps as usual and put them into my carrier bag, feeling the delicious anticipation of splashing around with my feet and ankles in the cool water.

I noticed something floating in the sea, about two yards from the water's edge. Oh dear! I thought. An empty bottle. Why don't people dispose of their rubbish at home, or in one of the public refuse bins! I waded towards the object, then I noticed it had some barnacles on it, but it was tightly sealed. I picked up the bottle by its neck. Looking into it where there was a gap in the barnacles, I could see a miniature of a ship in full sail. I gave a little gasp of astonishment and pleasure. How long has this been in the sea? I wondered. And how did it get there? Carefully now, I placed the bottle horizontally in the bottom of my carrier bag and brought it home. I put it on the kitchen table and sat looking at it for a long time. I know nothing about marine biology, but it seemed that the barnacles were stuck, although some green slime came away fairly easily when I gently used a baby wipe cloth. Now I could see more clearly the elaborate sails and rigging, it really was a work of art.

I took my magnifying glass from a draw to examine the miniature ship more closely. It had the words 'The Golden Hind' painted delicately in gold! I became more and more excited. So excited that I felt I had to share my find with someone. I telephoned my brother. He was intrigued. He suggested that I contact a maritime museum.

It was now Saturday evening, but on Sunday I visited Sidmouth Museum where I picked up some leaflets. These included information about Plymouth Museum, which is situated at Drake's Circus in Plymouth. Unfortunately that museum was to be closed on 27th August for refurbishment and not reopening until 2020, giving me little time. But on Tuesday 23rd August I went by bus and train to Plymouth, carrying my treasure very carefully.

When I reached the museum, I was lucky enough to be seen by the curator who showed great interest. He noticed something I had missed – there seemed to be a small roll of paper tucked inside the neck of the bottle. With infinite care he removed the cork, then drew out the paper with tweezers. By this time three or four people had gathered to see what was happening.

Now with a pair of tweezers in each hand, the curator gently spread out the roll of paper. It was yellow with age and nearly brittle but of good quality. In copperplate handwriting the message was clear. But he stood silently for a full minute in his astonishment. Then somewhat shakily he read aloud the following words.

'To whomsoever finds this, may it bring him good fortune in peace or in battle. Signed by the hand of Francis Drake, by the grace of God, Master of H.M. ship The Golden Hind. The year of Our Lord one thousand five hundred and ninety.'

2016